On The Mountain In The Morning

The politics of prose in healing

SHARON A WILDEY

Copyright © 2015 Rev. Sharon A. Wildey, Esq
All Rights Reserved.

"Fill us at daybreak with your kindness that we may shout for joy and gladness all our days."

– Psalm 90:14

Vagabond is on the mountain, on the top of the mountain, channeling Moses, wasting the time of blood sucking therapists, one on one with god, take it back, take it all back or move on god because I have had enough of Your help. I shout with clenched fists on the mountain and then the morning came and warmed me, gently at first, as I would not look at her.

On the mountain this morning the dawn spread herself across the entire horizon with her ever changing colors and patterns - her embrace slowing opening to me. As I fold myself into that embrace, I allow the possibility that this coming day could be the best one of my whole life. So for a moment I put aside my preconceived notions, my world of opinions, my grief and made way for her - welcomed her into my heart. Could be the best day of my whole life. Just could be.

On the mountain this morning, the sky begins to lighten and then lit up it moves on into day time. Every morning is reliable . . . predictable . . . every single day, without exception, it gives me the kind of peace that is palatable . . . noticeable. I can assume it . . . rely on its goodness. I can carry it with me into the day. I can feel it in my bones - my soul. Ancient therapy.

On the mountain this morning every little bird sitting in every tree and bush were singing their hearts out - singing out joyfully and full throated melodies known only to them and maybe Mozart. Even the morning timidly approached, like a late comer to symphony hall, bringing her most timid tinges of pale pink. Such respect the dawn and the birds have for a new day, new possibilities. Would that humanity have the same respect and find the courage to sit and sing each day into existence - taking a timid and courageous moment to consider all the infinite possibilities that come to us in the first moments of a new day.

On the mountain this morning, it is a cool, fleece jacket kind of sky, tinges of blues, greys and greens. I smell the richness of the coffee and hear the birds singing to the gift of the day. I pour the coffee and open the email and from a friend these words: "For God so loved the world that he gave his only son" and I hear my heart. Perhaps love is about sacrifice and perhaps we as a people on this small mountain this day need to love the world so much that we would give everything, absolutely everything. And then there is the rooster who is off key

Good Friday April 18, 2014

This morning on the mountain I stood on the edge of the mountain and watched the day in full light. I wondered where the morning had gone. Was she overcome by the mid-day and its busyness? Did her gentle presence of awaking humanity morph into impersonal movement - here and there - round about - car horns - commerce - babies crying. Or was she still there underneath it all - bearing witness to her creation and its eventual demise. My soul is like that - always present - bearing witness to what I have created, my busyness and my eventual demise.

On the mountain this morning I was awake early enough to open the kitchen window to the coolness of the night and noticed that the new day was a barely perceivable tinge of lightness on the horizon. I wouldn't know it was my new day if I hadn't experienced this sight before. Sometimes I think my life is like this, something new coming toward me, barely discernible and I don't always recognize it. Experience and trust become my teachers on this morning, seeing something barely seeable and knowing it will be good.

© Lee Gunter

On the mountain this morning it is predawn and silent except for a distant rooster barely discernible from the next mountain over. Neither sound nor light permeates the darkness. It has a stubbornness all of its own - a reluctance to loosen the cover of time and place – to see again. Sometimes I think there is a knowingness afoot with the dark - an intelligence born of witness to the adventures of humanity. So the eternal light comes with the rooster's crow, and humanity wakes, and so it goes . . .

*O*n the mountain this morning there are two volcanoes belching at me tossing their whiffs of smoke about - murmuring into the horizon. Bravely, I try and plan the day whilst worrying about the consequences of that volcano but I can no longer multi task. I used to multitask as my every day just to survive. But now, on this mountain, I am so devoid of subliminal stress my brain won't do it - plants its feet on the ground and simply refuses. I am so in tune with nature here, in tune with life and the occurrences of the ancient mornings. I don't care about the volcanoes or the tasks of the day, or whatever petty little annoyances the day has to bring me. Or mathematically said: Age = don't give a damn = Peace

On the mountain in the morning there is a moment, just a moment, when the mountains are framed with the most delicate pink, the sound of the birds is a bit louder, when I feel the morning is my friend, embracing me with kindness, allowing me to see and hear and feel, saying Good Morning my friend I love you. I am renewed.

This morning on the mountain, even the light moves a bit slower crossing the valley. The darn rooster missed his queue altogether and didn't rouse himself until quite late. There is nothing moving, not a sound, around the mountain. Perhaps the night was delayed by all the music, firecrackers, and fireworks bursting out all over the valley at midnight. Certainly it was loud and joyful; enough to hold back the night for a few minutes while history turned its page to another year. The sun really doesn't know or care that another year has begun, and personifying that great mass of fire doesn't make it intelligent. But then, personifying the new year doesn't make it less thrilling, less terrifying, or less expectant either. So I stand in the cool gray mist early this morning, letting the cats in and the dogs out, making the coffee, smelling the air and starting out peaceful. Starting out peaceful this new day - new year - I take a moment to wonder what fresh hell I will face in 2014, what fresh gift will come my way, what fresh . . .well, you get the drift. It's always a mix, and I am seventy years old.

On the mountain this morning, the skies are dark with ominous storm clouds, chilly, with a dampness in the air that seems to hang a bit deeper in the horizon. But suddenly, out of nowhere, the morning woke up and sent a shot of rose pink into the clouds shoving them aside like they were just smoke . . . plowing the road, she was. "Get out of the way," she demanded of the dark clouds, "I will bring the morning nurture to earth, and you need to get out of the way." And the dark clouds did just that. They got out of her way. And so she came showing her colors among the dark ones. The morning came . . . she did. Maybe it will rain later.

*O*n the mountain this morning I am awake earlier than usual, standing in the kitchen and allowing the silence of the mountain to grip me. And it does – simultaneously in the heart and gut. Not even a sound from the rooster penetrates the silence of the mountain at night . . . It feels solid - I walk into it blindly – a wall leading me to my "self" place, where all is real and abrupt and cold - where thoughts are too loud, plans for the day rude and out of place, where time is not present or even welcome - this place called absurdity maybe. Longing for the rooster to banish silence - Longing for the mountain to speak to me - Make me alive with your sounds. I think I may be dead

*T*his morning on the mountain as I stood anxiously waiting for the morning to make her appearance, I realized that she is just unpredictable. One day she bursts onto the scene with colors blazing. The next she is naughty and seductive. Sometime angry and sometimes lazy. Often she . . . well you get the picture. Oh Mother Morning, can't you just grow up, put on the uniform, be consistent, precise, on time and responsible. Really just being responsible would help. Why all these surprises? Every day we await your presence with trepidation. Such drama . . . people don't like drama. I suppose you know that.

On the mountain this morning, the morning lady threw her skirts across the sky splashing colors here and there with no regard for any order whatsoever. She didn't ask anyone's permission. Saucy and impertinent she brazenly gave no warning. Sashaying - leading with her shoulders. Flippant. Flirty. One minute it was dark and the next she knocked me over with her two-step. This is going to be some kind of day she whispered as she slowly stalked the rising sun - chasing him into the heavens for his audacity.

I wonder if the morning ages. I ask her today, do your colors ever fade? Your horizon wrinkle? And how about that promise of a new possibility - does it go unfulfilled? I ask her these questions this morning on the mountain as she lifted her eyes and peeked a bare thread of light onto the world. Then she stood, lifted her shoulders full up and with all her brightness she answered "Nope"

*O*n the mountain this morning the sky seems to say its Thanksgiving Day in the North as it is unusual for Costa Rica to start the day with grey skies and a bit of chill in the air. I take it as an approval of my decision to make this Thanksgiving my last one. I have been heroic in trying to find substitute happiness in the past several years without my family to cook for, to spend time with, and to laugh with. My family has always been blessed with a sense of humor. But they are gone and now I lamely try to find alternatives and substitutes for my time with them. I come away depressed and disappointed and find that I am just replacing my good memories with less than happy ones. It is almost like the substitute holidays were erasing the good times. So I have finally said, "No more". I will keep my good memories intact and stop trying to find peace, stop trying to be a Mom again, especially for those who no longer want me around and stop trying to be heroic. It is what it is. So today I will go to a gringo Thanksgiving with a hundred people I mostly don't know, try not to feel like I am going through a Salvation Army food line and put away the recipes, the laughter and the heartbreak. The last Thursday in November being just another day. I am going to tell the morning that tomorrow. She will understand. She has seen it before.

February 5

You can leave the mountain
But not the morning
The morning follows you
As gently as a mother's eye
All your life
The mother morning
Brings its infinite possibilities
At the slightest breaking of the night
Her stirring presence is waking
Just before our plans turn our face away
From her meaning
Nonetheless she is present
Nurturingly present
Every single day of our aging

This unique morning on the mountain showed the landscape dark as a silhouette against the pale blue sky. Heat lightning was flashing over the valley like an angry goddess ruminating about being awakened. My orange cat was lying low to the ground in the garden with her tail slowly swishing back and forth providing balance for the moment in which she will pounce on anything that might move. I am like that this day, low to the ground, looking to my history to provide balance, ready to pounce on whatever piece of joy comes my way. And, of course, relying on the promise of morning that a piece of joy will come my way and I will capture it and I will cherish it . . . like my orange kitty . . . toying with the idea.

I took my broken soul
up to the mountain
Channeling Moses
I went to the mountain
top
and cried out to God
The ashes of what was
my heart rested in my
jeans pocket
The bits of self mingled
with the scars of my
achievements
in my hand
I cried out to God
To send the Angel for
me
That I had no desire to
love again
Instead God sent the
vultures
I saw them from the
cliff
Soaring black animals
heading for me
They snatched my
ashes, my cries and my
deep desire
from my hand
They mocked my
achievements
Reducing me to
ancientness
And then, these great
black carrions played
in the sky
Throwing bits of my
leftovers here and
there
While I watched in
surprise
For a moment I hated
Hated the vultures,
God, the Angel
Then the Angel came
But it was too late
The hatred had passed
The vultures came
back for me
To teach me to soar on
the winds of life
Without shame
The pure air filling my
lungs
I played with them all
day
The fields were green
The soil rich with
promise
I went to the mountain
To channel Moses
I stayed there
I lived again
The vultures soared
and disappeared
Moses smiled
And then I went home

On the mountain in the morning, walking along a dirt road at first light near Casa de Ana, I heard the coffee pickers, mostly families from Nicaragua, singing, laughing and talking. The time is ripe for harvest. Trucks full of coffee pickers have been at their task for several weeks and bags of the precious beans sit alongside the road waiting for an eager market. The air is heavily weighted with the smell of the husks blown off the beans mixed with the smell of smoke from the burning sugar cane fields' subtlety adding variety to the otherwise clean and fresh breeze. Men were cutting the cane with machetes as I walked by them they waved and smiled. And I smiled and waved back to them. A bit later down the road, I realized that I was not in fear – walking alone, along an isolated dirt road, in a foreign county, men with long sharp knives that could cut me in half, rape me, steal. In fact it did not occur to me to be afraid or even cautious. I stopped for a minute to catch my breath and then began to cry. I cried deeply for my country and the death dealing fears that are lived every moment there and passed on to the children. Returning home as the morning was up in the midday sky I reflected. The morning seemed to understand.

This morning on the mountain I chose to open myself completely to the promises of the morning. It is a choice. That thought came to me a few days ago when I realized that I always hold part of myself back from nearly everything and everyone. My insight came when a lavender tea rose that I had planted bloomed. I appreciated the rose deeply and was excited to see it on the bank behind the casa. I felt satisfied by it as an achievement having planted it myself, watered it, fed it, and talked to it. A tinge of emptiness came when I felt that there was more being offered by this delicate lavender being, and I couldn't seem to reach it. So today, I waited on the morning. I stood perfectly still with my bare arms outstretched, my chest uplifted, and my chin tilted upwards. And when the morning began her descent into my space I closed my eyes. I felt her movement slowly up my body; the warmth was poetic as it climbed up to my face intensifying with each moment. I started to speak, but she said, "Shh." I knew then that she loved me, and I did not have to speak. So on that day, I became the lavender tea rose.

April 13

This morning on the mountain started suddenly with a splatter of peach and deep purples where the gray rain clouds will eventually develop, but for now was contained by a muted sky of blue across the horizon. It was as if some ancient god just randomly threw some colors out of the heavens. Caught unaware, I ran outside to see this water color painting knowing that it would last only minutes. In the distance, roosters on the mountains were calling out to each other fulfilling their historical obligation to announce a new day. The breeze was stronger than usual creating a rustling sound among the citrus trees and spreading the subtle smell of oranges. The twinkling lights of the town in the distance began to fade in the new light. As I stood proudly although diminished by the magnificence of nature, I prayed for a renewed sense of compassion toward other human beings and especially those members of my family. I prayed for strength and insight and peace. I prayed for my friends whose beauty is the only beauty that compares to the morning sky. I stood observing this magic moment of beauty and granted quietly to myself that I had seen something worth remembering.

*I*n the pre-morning darkness I wake and turn on the light, and the rooster crows. It is our habit now. It is as if we are bonded to this ritual. One morning, this morning actually, I decided to irritate the rooster, so I didn't turn on the light. True to my plan, he did not wake up and crow. When the morning came, she noticed that the rooster was still asleep, so she, the morning, cleared her throat softly, and with that, the rooster jumped out of his feathers! He raced across the yard squawking his upset to the other animals who were getting a bit of pleasure from the entire scene as I was. Finally he settled down and began to apologize to the morning, blaming me for not turning on the light. "Silly bird," said the morning, "I was before you always." "Your crowing is not because the human turns on the light." "My coming is not because you crow." "Foolish bird - that is why humans eat you."

April 17

Sitting at the computer this morning trying to compose, I realized the raucous noise blasting into the house was a sum total of the rooster, the calf, the dogs, and the yellowish green bird who scolds the cats every morning. I gave up and went into the living room where I was greeted by the biggest honking spider that I have ever seen. My cats saw it at the same time and immediately turned tail and went outside. See if they get any treats today! I didn't know if the spider was harmless, so I followed the cats out of the room - with a lot more dignity however. Right then Edgar knocked on the window to give me some fruit and assured me the spider was harmless. I guess that means non-poisonous. Certainly the thing is not harmless. I went back to the computer now that every living thing in the area has had its say except me. So I begin to compose: I LOVE THIS COUNTRY!

On the veranda this morning, taking in the clear view across the valley where a rainbow was hanging gently over the mountains to the south, I wondered how many rainbows I had missed by not looking up and out from my desk. So I began to look out, and up, and down the hill, and further over to the other mountain. I saw rainbows forming their arcs starting at the base and moving upward. Sometimes there were double rainbows on top of each other and some had different colors and hues and.... Well you see where this is going. I am either a person sitting at my desk writing about creation or I am a person who can BEHOLD.

On the mountain this morning, right after church, my neighbors began to walk down the lane toward the fence where the new vaca had been placed the day before. They all exclaimed as to his beauty and playfully petted his ears. They all came - children, the grandmothers and the brothers. For me, I now add another instrument for the symphony of morning sounds . . . the soft mooing of the vaca. He often came to the fence and looked at me with big calf eyes - sweet and innocent. Then I realized what that little vaca was being penned up for, his destiny was right before my eyes. I bolted straight up from my desk and ran to his pen. I looked around and made sure no one was watching and then I whispered in his ear, "Run away!" I say it to him two or three times a week when no one is watching.

This morning on the mountain, I stand at my kitchen window beating eggs into the batter of my chocolate macaroon cake. It is dominoes day with the girls, pool for the guys, and it is my unique gift to prepare the cake. It is so early, I again am blessed to watch the wondrous morning peek over the mountain, slowly imposing her distaff self on the landscape. Today it is mostly blues as great waves of gray are pushed aside giving way to her royal presence. I realize she is beginning to prepare food for her loved ones as well; rain and sun. Food, as love, yearning to love today.

September 23

I eagerly awaited the morning today as I was full of an idea. When she appeared, I said to her that perhaps I should learn to play the cello or trumpet, certainly not the tuba or drums, and the flute or violin takes way too much time to learn. Perhaps more time than I have. Well, I say this because I have been thinking about the end times, all year really, and thinking I should make one last grand effort to take a stand for happiness. I am convinced I have found a comfortable place where I can live it all out alongside my issues kept in check, alongside my resources, or what's left of them. I can even go from day to day without too much trauma, that is, unless I still care about politics or religion, and then, well I am on my own. I am proposing here that if I take a turn to the left or the right, it really doesn't matter as long as it is a turn away from what I have now, then maybe I might have a glorious experience. Well, I was nearly out of breath when I finished explaining this great idea of the cello and turning left or right. The morning smiled patiently as she listened politely and then went on about her job bringing light to the valley. When she was just a bit away from me, I heard this laugh - a kind of precious laugh - an amused laugh. Well, anyway, I heard the laugh all day. I wonder how she did that.

This morning on the mountain, I am sipping a hot cup of Costa Rican coffee, sitting on the veranda, getting "the bad face" from black cat because I am petting orange kitty instead of him. Reflecting on the celebration of gratitude yesterday at the home of Joyce and Anthony, I realize how fascinating Americans are when they are away from the continent. We were a group of about thirty people from all faiths, economic circumstances, education levels, philosophies, and several different states and cities. The common denominator, I think, was our individual desire to live in peace and kindness with each other, our planet and our souls. The place, the food, the common good - so grateful after a lifetime of the reality that I fled.

This morning on the mountain
Will I ever see you again, I ask
Will you still use the same shades of pink to mark the day
When I am gone or
Will you just creep up over the mountain
And not worry much about your display
Will you look for me at first light
Or bother not
Do you think the rooster will still crow
For me, even when I am beyond its call
Or will it just sigh and get on with business
I am sure I will miss you morning
Where ever there is a day to begin
A whisper to hear
Or a heart to soothe

*O*n the mountain this morning, there is no light save for the dimness of the gray fog that has blanked out human existence. The mountains, the valley, and even the garden have been replaced with a shadowy replica of a bad movie. Everything is saturated - living things and man made things - in primal wet. Nothing is visible, and there is silence except for the constant dripping of the drainage pipe from the roof which seems to run eternally. Even the cats sit on the edge of the veranda seemingly uneasy given the transformation of their morning world. Realizing there is nothing to see or hear, we quickly return to the safety of our house where the smell of coffee seems to make the only familiar statement of our known world. Nature has claimed this day, and we have no vote in the matter. We are sent inside, to our rooms, as if we are errant children. Today I will need to hide from the nature I came here to love, to reassess my presence here, to believe again that yes, there will be light again, and soon. And yes, the rain will stop in three weeks as it always does here in paradise. Meanwhile, I stare out the window and try to remember better times.

March 9

On the mountain this morning, it seems the dawn is being thrown out of the universe with a wild abandon splattering peaches and bluish grays landing where they may on the country sky as if the morning had to get it done, get it on the table, hurry up and move on. Even the rooster's crow is a bit sharpened and short. Nonetheless I watched the few minutes it took for the dawn to crack the night time. I missed it yesterday; the day was full of an earthquake and ambulance rides carrying friends and a neighbor who needed fennel seeds. All of this occurred without the comfort of my friend, the morning. Well, today I am here watching the universe, and even though you are throwing the morning colors on the table in a haphazard way, I am here, and here I find my being.

On the mountain this morning, I am awake earlier than usual, standing in the kitchen allowing the silence of the mountain to grip me. Not even a sound from the rooster penetrates the silence of the mountain at night. It feels solid - I walk into it blindly - a wall leading me to my self-place, where all is real and abrupt and cold, where thoughts are too loud, plans for the day, rude and out of place, where time is not present or even welcome....this place absurdity. I am longing for the rooster to banish the night's silence, longing for the mountain to speak to me.

You can say goodbye to the mountain
But not to the morning
She is an old woman
Putting one foot in front of the other
Getting on with the day …..life maybe
Too wise to care about the issues of the day
Too old to be frightened
She is just there …..everyday
Nodding to you
Doing what she does

On the mountain this morning there is a sense of wetness all around me. You can smell it, see it, and taste it in the air. Even the birds are a little quieter this morning and the darn pesky rooster is still hiding under the porch. It is the kind of wetness that nature can dump on you with just one bang of thunder and one lightning flash. Without warning the dark clouds suddenly jump over the mountain range like a small child carrying a pail of water to show her Mommy, tripping and spilling her precious contents all over the grown-ups in the valley. I have never seen so much rain water in one sitting, gushing out of the gutters, running off the hills in breakneck speed. People are taught by their environment - at least human people are taught that way. We learn to dig deep ditches and create space in our lives for that much water to run off into the rivers. We are safe because we live cooperatively with our thunder, lightning and water. This morning I am appreciating that relationship.

On the mountain this morning I awoke earlier than usual, around 4:30, giving the rooster an opportunity to bravely sound off and then go back to sleep -- unusual for the pesky bird. Black cat took it as an opportunity to get a bonus petting jumping on my lap closing his eyes and enjoying his ears and neck being rubbed. I followed my usual routine of brushing my teeth and making coffee and turning on the internet. It all caused me to think about morning rituals and how always my brain directs me to ritualized thinking about the day and what has to be accomplished like getting apples for Sidney's birthday apply cake. Then what to worry about: I trudge up worries that I have carried around for some months, then those I carry around for some weeks and then, of course, what can I worry about today. Years of child rearing and working in troublesome professions have carved out their space in my brain. The habits created then stay with me and demand their time and space. Perhaps today I will create some new ones. I will start off the day, after coffee of course when the day really starts, I will start off the day thinking about my blessings, my friends, thoughts of love and kindness and mercy. I think I will avoid the news for a while and think of my *sailor friend out on the ocean separated from his precious family or my friend in the hospital or my neighbors corn crop. It is time for some new rituals -- ones that I deserve and ones that will gently lead me into the day. Deserving – an unexplored thought.*

On the mountain this morning – an ever so slight appearance of light. The rooster sounds its warning that a new light is approaching with its intent to write upon my history of days. I sense the approach and feel awed by my youthfulness. Who am I, after all, to stand here before history and count myself as old when the very air I breathe was here from the beginning of Time. Whatever preordained mission this new light brings near in this moment of transition, I am merely a witness to that which once was only an ancient possibility. I realize my pensiveness about this as I try and make out wthe thin line barely tracing the clouds in the night sky. I search for just a hint of the memory to come – to brace myself I say. Unaware of this human foolishness, the rooster unashamedly continues to sound the morning alarm. That bird simply doesn't get it.

*J*une 21th. The morning came sadly on the mountain today. She didn't display her usual colors or swirl herself about choosing instead to amble in rather quietly. As I watched she to seemed to pause, to wait a moment. I looked at her intently trying to burn her memory into my soul for a while and then when the light was just right I walked in the garden around my house for the last time. I planted every flower in that garden but still it was only in the spring time of its becoming. My feet were damp from the tears of the morning having fallen softly on the earth. My yellow bushes puffed their little chests out as I walked by wanting me to be proud of them and I was. And oh, look there - my white rose bush blushing its tips with pink shot out 3 blooms from yesterday. I think it is my going away bouquet. I see the 4 o'clock that Corrine gave me and the struggling planter that belonged first to Anna and then Corrine and now me. It seemed to be saying "I'm OK - Really." The tree with the floppy white blossoms looked like an old fashioned Easter hat. That tree was planted 2 years ago and twice taken down to one leaf by the cutter ants. Survivor, I said to it and the tree just smiled and lifted its chin proudly. On the red stone path now I see the weeds that have heckled and bullied me for two years. Those weeds are only good for compost, I think, as I crush them under foot. I didn't need to do that as they are someone else's problem now. But I wanted to.

Finally I step onto the terrazzo and look to the east one last time trying to imprint upon my heart the picture of the valley and the mountain. The view that had so comforted me all these months. Peaceful and reassuring its presence always calmed me down. A cold nose touches my leg and I look down and find Moses and Aaron sitting quietly beside me taking in the view as well. They didn't sleep well last night. I think they knew that their Mommy was leaving them today. I feel their spirits and they mine in that moment. Leaving people whom I love is I guess my destiny and dogs are people as we all know. I don't know if I can leave them. My heart breaks and I cannot look at them again.

The morning warmth is on my back now. It feels like a hand on my shoulder steadying me. Just then I feel the cool indifference of the evening - looking west. I have always preferred the warmth of the morning but the evening has always beckoned to me. Now I turn toward it as I sigh a goodbye. I am leaving my sandals here but taking my poems - even those that no one reads. I leave my power here as well – that power that I found among the comings and goings, the losses and gains, the parties, the food and the friends and the enemies. I no longer need to manage my course. I am engaged and locked into the cool indifference of the evenings. It is where I am going now.

Edgar comes with a last hug and Pablo arrives and loads up the 3 suitcases of 7 years of living. He decides to take the back road to the airport for which I thank him for a last glimpse of the unique beauty of this country. Eddy is with him and so I am among people who care for me. I declare to myself that having people who care for me is an achievement worth remembering.

Within a brief time, I find myself sitting next to an unshaven Texan who ordered white wine for breakfast. There is always that part of life that seems to find me everywhere - the truly ridiculous - from which I often find humor. He calls me "Mam" and helps me with my tray table. I wondered if he would have called me "Mam" if he had seen me at 25. It is ok though.

Ascending now I am watching the last of the lushness fade from my view as it secrets itself under the puffy white clouds and the highway of change. Finally I can see no more and the *connection is gone, I think that I have cherished every second of it as if it was my last knowing. So I leave again, another journey - another place. On my way to becoming an unavoidable Being . . . searching always searching*

There is always a sunset and a sunrise. It is there for you. Don't get in the way of that.

- From the movie WILD

*S*haron Ann Wildey is an experienced lawyer, ordained minister, conflict mediator, teacher, writer and poet. She graduated from Indiana University with a BA in Forensic Science and a Law degree (JD). Later in life she obtained a Masters of Divinity from Chicago Theological Seminary and was ordained in the United Church of Christ.

She is the author of "Abandoned Parents: The Devil's Dilemma" available on Amazon. Her next book is titled "Abandoned Parents: Healing Beyond Understanding" due out in October, 2015.

You can find her on Facebook.

*

Heartfelt thanks is given to Karen Andersen, Lydia H. Hall for editing, Margarita Persico for comments and support and Ann Silverman, Mark Bean and Nancy Paradisco for their continued nurture and patience, oh god, what patience

Manufactured by Amazon.ca
Acheson, AB